S0-AYE-181

Great Britain
Classical Art Tours
Westminster Abbey

Claudio Gorlier

WARNER MEMORIAL LIBRARY
EASTERN UNIVERSITY
ST. DAVIDS, PA 19087-3696

11/10/08

NA 5470 .W5 G6713 1982
Gorlier, Claudio.
Westminster Abbey

Translated by Eurolingua, Professional Language Services Ltd,
15-16 Newman Street, Oxford Street, London W1P 3HD

Original title: L'Abbazia di Westminster

Chief editors of ,,Classical Art Tours":
Silvio Locatelli und Marcello Boroli

© Manfred Pawlak Verlagsgesellschaft mbH, Herrsching
Distributed in the UK by Hawk Books Ltd

© Instituto Geografico de Agostini SpA, Novara

»Heroes and kings, your distance keep!«

Morality, behold and fear!
What a change of flesh is here:
Think how many royal bones
Sleep within these heaps of stones:
Here they lie, had realms and lands,
Who now want strength to stir their hands.
Here, from their pulpits seal's with dust,
They preach, »In greatness is no trust!«
Here's an acre sown indeed,
With the richest royallest seed,
That the earth did e'er drink in,
Since the first man died for sin.
(Francis Beaumont, *Westminster Abbey*)

Perhaps this poem by the Elizabethan playwright, Beaumont (himself buried in the abbey), creates the most memorable image of the classical, royal mausoleum, an emblem of the continuity of order and the disturbing mystery of death. Its significance as a »national sanctuary« taking shape over the centuries becomes clear if we consider two other factors: the investiture of kings and, with the tombs, the legitimisation of the fame of great men, itself the quintessence of a country's spirit. From this point of view, the abbey becomes a focal point, a true microcosm, and so it is better to forego commemorative rhetoric and concentrate on the eventful history which it literally embodies and often dramatically reflects.

Westminster Abbey was created at a fairly critical juncture in English history, which legend has obligingly tried to minimise. King Edward the Confessor of England acceded to the throne in 1042 after a period of exile. He was continually having to deal with revolts by the great feudal lords as well as Scotland. He decided to construct a Benedictine monastery incorporating a great church, intending to erect an extraordinary new monument, and chose a »central« location for particular political reasons. His residence was nearby, on the island which the Saxons called Thorney, in the marshland between the rivulets which flowed into the Thames. Even during the Middle Ages, this island served a so-called institutional purpose distinct from commercial London. A devotee of St. Peter, the king constructed the abbey on the ruins of a church which had been consecrated to the apostle. It took at least fifteen years to build and was consecrated on 28th December 1065. The king was too ill to attend the ceremony and died on 5th January 1066. In fact, Edward had already prepared his sepulchre, which has been venerated over the centuries in all its various states.

For reasons of convenience, tradition has made Edward a paragon of religious piety and healthy living. There is no proof, however, or perhaps it was later that the abbot Osbert expediently concocted these astute falsehoods which were used by Henry II to canonise Edward the Confessor in 1161. If anything, historical fact shows Edward to have been an important thread of continuity. Although his mother was Norman and he was educated in Normandy (the abbey reflects this style and Norman architects and labourers were certainly used for building it), in practice he was the final link in a chain of Saxon kings and seemed to resemble them in appearance. The court itself was fundamentally Saxon, as was the language he spoke. He left no heirs however, and a few months later his successor, Harold, crowned at Westminster, went into battle at Hastings and was beaten by the invading Norman army under the command of William the Conqueror.

The solemn coronation of William I, on Christmas Day 1066, was, therefore, the first great turning-point to be sanctioned at Westminster. Even though William the Conqueror boasted family ties with Edward (cousin by marriage), he began a new cycle, not only historical but also cultural, when we think of the profound impression which the Normans left on the English language, the so-called »Middle English«. William was crowned in accordance with the ancient Saxon ritual of acclamation, which produced moments of panic and disorder among the king's Norman followers, marshalled outside the abbey. From that time on, all the kings of England have been crowned at Westminster, with the exceptions of Edward V, the boy who was murdered by his usurping uncle, Richard III, and Edward VIII who reigned for one year, in 1936, before abdicating.

While the abbey was being extended to include the adjacent monarchs' residences (these extensions and additions continued until the eighteenth century, creating a permanent building site), English history was suffering an incessant period of internal conflict and foreign wars. Henry II, founder of the Angevin empire, canonised Edward the Confessor but began a bitter clash with the Church which culminated in 1170 with the killing of Archbishop Thomas Becket in Canterbury Cathedral. Henry III, as refined as his father, John Lackland, was aggressive, was none the less resolute in his battle against the rebelling feudal lords whom he defeated, but he was humiliated by having to respect the Magna Carta. He paid enormous attention to the abbey and, as the driving force behind Edward the Confessor's memorial chapel and the great Chapter House, was largely responsible for the appearance of the abbey as we know it today. Henry III's son, Edward I, completed the project by bringing back the marble for his father's tomb from the Crusades and, having beaten the Scottish, the fabulous Stone of Scone on which the Celtic kings were traditionally crowned. Westminster did not escape the terrible Black Death of 1348 which decimated the monks and slowed down completion of the great nave. In 1381, the Peasants' Revolt shook the country, which was involved in the mounting Hundred Years' War. During troubled meditation at Edward the Confessor's tomb, Richard II's personal tragedy ended when his cousin, Count Bolingbroke, who succeeded him with the name of Henry IV, hired an assassin to murder him. He was buried in the abbey next to his wife, Anne of Bohemia and here literature and unforgiving historical fact become interwoven as we think of Shakespeare's character, Richard, and then Henry, the subtle politician tormented by power struggles and shadows from the past. Henry IV did not keep his promise to atone for his sins by leading a crusade, but grimly fulfilled the prophecy of his death in the Holy City by dying, at night and in front of the fire, in the *Jerusalem Chamber* of the abbey. Shakespeare relates the story in *Henry IV, part II*. His son, Henry V, perhaps the most popular king at that time and certainly in Shakespeare's *Histories*, anxiously kept vigil at Westminster before his coronation. Yet his father, probably to avoid any unfortunate proximity to Richard II, was buried not at Westminster but at Canterbury. Henry V, victor at Agincourt, died in France when he was thirty-five. His brother stated sadly but proudly that he was too great to live long. A magnificent funeral procession took two months to carry his body to the abbey. The year was 1422.

Chaucer, the First »Commoner« in the Kings' Memorial Chapel

In the year 1400, Geoffrey Chaucer was buried in the southern transept of the church. He was one of the very first commoners and the first poet to receive such an honour. As time passed, the transept became *Poets' Corner,* one of Westminster's best-known features. Curiously, rather than as a homage to his prestige as a poet, Chaucer was buried in the abbey because he passed the latter years of his life there finishing the *Canterbury Tales* in a building which was later demolished to make room for Henry VII's chapel. Burial in the abbey did not become a proper tribute to literary merit until Elizabethan times.

Elizabeth also came to the throne after one of the most troubled periods in English history, well-represented by the issues surrounding the abbey. In fact, there seemed to be no break between the bloody civil struggle in the Wars of the Roses and the Hundred Years' War. For this reason, the coronation of Richard III, usurper of the English throne, can be considered on the whole to be the most dramatic because of its chilling ambiguity. The ceremony had been prepared for the legitimate heir, Edward V. However, the boy was imprisoned in the Tower of London by his uncle, who replaced him and received the crown in a ceremony overstated in its splendour but none the less hurried, which amounted to a coup d'état. Edward V was assassinated in the tower. Richard III died in battle in 1485, and the civil war ended with Henry VII's accession to the throne. He was crowned at Westminster in the same year (but secretly since Cardinal Bourchier laid claim to Canterbury's seniority) and the Tudor dynasty began.

Thus we reach another crossroads in the history of England and Westminster Abbey. Under Henry VIII, who succeeded his father Henry VII in 1509, the English Reformation began. Henry VIII was crowned in splendour at Westminster, which had now been embellished with the chapel for Henry VII and his queen. Naturally the new king, claiming ties to the Roman Church, concerned himself with increasing the abbey's prestige and importance. In fact, in 1515, he officially granted Westminster the right of a cardinal. The mitre was received by Thomas Wolsey, the last great political prelate of medieval England. Only his death, caused by illness in 1530, saved him from trial for high treason after becoming one of the most influential men in the kingdom.

Wolsey's death opened the way to breaking away from Rome and Henry VIII played the major rôle in this. If the Reformation caused some bitter ups and downs for the Westminster monks, who had been deprived of power and twice driven out, it also raised the abbey's standing enormously, to the level of official recognition by the king as a cathedral headed by a bishop and a dean. Although the abbey had always held a civic as well as a religious rôle, the Anglican reform's affirmation of a religion with the king as its leader secularised it totally.

It was then that it truly became a State institution. With Catholicism banished and Thomas More sent to the gallows, Westminster reached its zenith. The Reformation naturally brought about the dissolution of the abbey's traditional structure and the expulsion of the monks. Some went into exile, some to prison and some were put to death for their active opposition to the Reformation. Furthermore, images believed to be objects of idolatry were abolished, which had bad repercussions even on the sepulchre of Edward the Confessor. However, the monks accepted their inevitable defeat and officially signed a document of renunciation accepting the transfer of power. The library was dispersed and the old mass-books adapted to the new liturgy.

Henry VIII was buried at Windsor. He was preoccupied by the problem of who should succeed him and had arranged for the coronation of his young and sickly son, Edward VI, so named in honour of Edward the Confessor. The boy, who was born during the king's third marriage to Jane Seymour, was not able to stand up for the ceremony, the gloomiest and most pathetic to have taken place in the cathedral. Edward VI inherited the throne in 1547, when he was nine years old. He died in 1553 and was buried next to his grandfather, Henry VII, in the Renaissance chapel by Pietro Torrigiano, defined *orbis miraculum* and destined to suffer iconoclastic attacks from the Puritans. The English Reformation prayer book was used for the first time at his funeral.

Mary Tudor (Mary the Catholic or Bloody Mary as the Protestants called her) was the wife of Philip of Spain and was crowned in the abbey, to her now irreparably violated. She persecuted the Protestants mercilessly. (Among her victims was Archbishop Cranmer who, according to the chronicles, had held the dying Henry VIII's hand.) The queen was desperately afraid that the holy oil had lost its power and that the coronation seat no longer held any sacred power. Before the ceremony she had the chapels washed thoroughly with soap and water, holy oil sent by the Bishop of Arras and a new chair blessed by the Pope. Edward the Confessor's memorial chapel was rebuilt, the monastery re-opened to the Benedictine monks and mass was celebrated in Latin. It was a short-lived restoration. Mary died in 1558 after England's ruinous defeat in France and the loss of Calais. The twenty-five year old Elizabeth acceded to the throne and the last vestiges of Catholicism disappeared. Abbot Feckenham, who did not accept the new liturgy and regal supremacy, was persuaded to suppress his feelings with the promise of promotion. However, some accounts suggest that when the queen sent for him, he simply remained in the garden planting elms. It was well and truly over the Benedictines. The queen announced that »due to the inspiration of divine clemency and the true religion ... this monastery must be reformed and returned to its original state of genuine and brotherly love«.

A Centre of Learning

Westminster entered the Modern Age with the Charter signed by Elizabeth in 1560. Despite some adaptations, this document has governed the abbey to the present day. Westminster gained broader powers and prestigious privileges, so becoming an extraordinary centre of learning. It is worth noting that Westminster School became Westminster College, one of the country's most important centres of learning together with Christ Church in Oxford and Trinity Church in Cambridge. It is easy to understand how this became possible when religious institutions were secularised. From then on, the abbot and the dean were usually great scholars. Meanwhile, the building was making new progress and at the beginning of the sixteenth century the influential Abbot Islip began constructing the two west towers.

The queen must have been aware of this new life-blood when she came by river in a long procession to be crowned in the abbey. After Ben Jonson, many famous students attended the school and there was a particularly active cultural life within the abbey walls, although in fact this was nothing new. William Caxton, the great printer and the first to publish books in English, had already established his workshop in the abbey at the end of the fifteenth century. The prominent position attributed to literature and the arts explains and justifies the use of the south transept, acknowledged as *Poets' Corner.* One could see the burial of Edmund Spenser in 1599 as the ideal starting point. He was one of the major English poets and author of *The Faerie Queen.* The honour then fell to Ben Jonson. In considering the importance of epitaphs placed on tombs, one should add that the great playwright has been given the most concise and epigrammatic yet also the most unfortunate epitaph. The stonecutter, obviously not well versed in literature, made an irreparable mistake by inserting one *h* too many: »*O rare Ben Johnson!*« Then Drayton and Beaumont took their places. Today Shakespeare would also come to mind, but literary and political Elizabethan society did not grant him any special recognition. On the contrary, and paradoxically, Westminster does not house the tomb of the supreme protagonist of English literature.

Elizabeth was buried in the abbey a month after her death, in 1603, with a funeral of great ceremony. It was also so intensely dramatic that one influential person observed: »No-one can remember ever seeing anything of this kind«. There is yet another paradox in the history of Westminster: the queen was buried next to her sister Mary, her enemy and persecutor, and both with a contritely conciliatory Latin inscription: *»Regno consortes et urna, hic obdormimus Elizabetha et Maria sorores, in spe resurrectionis.«* (Consorts on the throne and in the tomb, here sleep the sisters Elizabeth and Mary, hoping for resurrection.) In 1612 Elizabeth's successor, James I, son of Mary Stuart, who had been condemned to death by the queen, completed the reconciliation, or rather took his revenge, by moving his mother's remains to Westminster, but his coronation was a quieter event, because the plague had once more struck London and, immediately after the coronation, he hurriedly left the city, moving to Windsor and Winchester. His attempts were in vain for the plague followed the court implacably.

The coronation of the first Stuart king is also important because of the personality of the officiating abbot, later promoted to dean. He was Lancelot Andrewes, one of the leading figures of English culture at the beginning of the seventeenth century and the main author of the basic »authorised version« of the Bible. After the coronation, and while the plague raged, killing thirty five thousand Londoners, Andrewes withdrew along the Thames to Chiswick with his collaborators to make nature studies of the fields, cattle and water. According to his own statements, he derived great pleasure and joy from these activities. The new natural sciences, illustrated in Bacon's epistemology, had a considerable effect on Westminster.

The Triumph of Music

The years preceding the Puritan revolution were marked by intense activity in the abbey. Musical interest was intensified and became one of its characteristic features. Orlando Gibbons, appointed organist, was one of the greatest composers of his time and this tradition continued until the end of the century with Henry Purcell, the greatest name in English musical history. However, as always, there were gloomy and tragic aspects to the life of the abbey. Detained in its *Gatehouse Prison* was Walter Raleigh, a poet and politician who colonised Virginia, and a gentleman quite close to Elizabeth, in fact one of her favourites. When James I sentenced him to death, Raleigh went to the gallows accompanied by the dean, and his stoic death ended a career which was full of contrasting light and shadow.

The second Stuart king, Charles I, was condemned to death and beheaded by Oliver Cromwell's revolutionaries and the abbey was not spared in this wave of Puritan rigour. The renewed iconoclasm, made furious attacks on the many contents considered to be too ostentatious and heathen, including Henry VII's chapel. Cromwell's troops literally camped in the abbey and caused substantial damage, demonstrating their contempt. In 1643, for example, two companies of soldiers who were quartered in the cathedral burned church furnishings from the altars and smashed the organs, selling the pipes in exchange for large supplies of beer. One should point out however, that information about the worst desecration, including the use of the abbey as a brothel, came from anti-Cromwell libellists and should be viewed with some suspicion. The fact remains that, like the centres of power, the centres of learning during this period of very real cultural revolution had moved elsewhere, with another major English literary figure – John Milton – as one of its leading figures. Life in the abbey had now become almost clandestine, or was limited to meetings organised by the Puritans who had imposed their Calvinist code.

With the Restoration, the abbey, a conservative and realist establishment, regained its former strength, and not without vendetta. Dean Sprat wanted to erase the memory of Milton altogether, and only much later was a tombstone in Westminster granted to acknowledge him, so for very different reasons, the tombs of the two giants in English literature, Shakespeare and Milton, were never to be placed in Westminster. As some compensation, the coronation of Charles II, with all its pomp and ceremony, clearly symbolised the return of absolute monarchy. On the whole, the upper echelons of the abbey's clergy whose political stance unreservedly betrayed Tory sympathies were not displeased since they themselves were recovering from the humiliating conditions which they had suffered. Here history and literature mingle once again. The most observant and lively information about Charles II's coronation comes from the two best-known diaries of the century, those of Samuel Pepys and John Evelyn, both great writers and great gossips. Pepys in particular was inclined to be obsessed with the appearance of things to the point of fascination with the macabre. History seemed to go back in time, cancelling out the years of Cromwell's Commonwealth just as the statesman's mortal remains, which had been in the abbey for two years, had been removed. Archbishop Juxton, who officiated at the coronation, had helped Charles I onto the gallows.

The foundations of the Restoration were far more fragile than they appeared however, and the fine balance was upset with James II, brother and successor of Charles II. The king, who suddenly died in February 1685, excusing himself for what amounted almost to be an irrational act of disloyalty, allowed his brother to persuade him *in extremis* to convert to Catholicism. The funeral rites were performed furtively, at night, with the honours reduced to a minimum (»in great obscurity«, Evelyn writes). James attended with a small group of peers, and the deceased was placed in Henry VII's chapel, not far from some of his illegitimate children, who had died before him.

James II's coronation was not only a quiet affair but also curtailed because of his adherence to Catholicism and his marriage to a Catholic Italian princess. The central part, the Communion, was eliminated from the service and, according to witnesses, the king was stern and distant while his wife participated with great devotion. During preparations for the ceremony, an unforeseen event took place. On the same day that the Duke of Monmouth, the Protestant rival to the succession, embarked to head an armed revolt which was crushed within a few weeks and ended with his capture, trial and beheading, a wooden structure in the abbey fell on Edward the Confessor's memorial chapel and smashed the coffin. Charles Taylor, a chorister with an interest in antiques, took the crucifix and a gold chain which, with the dean's consent, he offered to the king as a relic from the saint. James II kept them even during his exile, at least according to his *Memoirs*, although the truth remains in question.

The crucial year of 1688 marked the fall of James II and the accession of William of Orange who had, like William the Conqueror, landed on English shores. The constitutional monarchy began and was later consolidated by the Hanoverian dynasty. Bearing in mind the irreconcilable friction between the Catholic king and the Anglican Church, William must have been welcomed at Westminster, for James had resolutely and insensitively distanced himself to the extent of building a Catholic chapel in Whitehall, designed by the great architect Christopher Wren (who rebuilt London after the fire in 1666, designed St Paul's Cathedral and completed the towers of Westminster). Even the powerful dean, Thomas Sprat, the refined man of letters and staunch monarchist conservative, did not welcome the »Glorious

Revolution« gladly. The ambiguity of his political tance troubled him on the eve of his death, in 1710, but he stood his ground honourably. In fact, the coronation of William III and his queen, Mary, daughter of James II, was affected by the conflicts in the bishopric and among the higher echelons of the Anglican clergy. Again Evelyn writes that »much of the splendour of the ceremony was diminished by the absence of clergy who should have been officiating, with only five bishops and five judges present and with many noblemen and ladies missing.« Furthermore, there remained the painful memory of the plague of 1664. It was imaginatively recreated in the eighteenth century by Defoe in his Journal of the Plague, which had killed seventy thousand people, and the fire of 1666 which left one hundred thousand homeless.

At the end of 1694, a smallpox epidemic claimed new victims, one of them the very popular Queen Mary. An enormous crowd attended her funeral, lining the streets leading to the abbey, where Henry Purcell's funeral music was played. A year later, the same music was played at the composer's own funeral. He died when he was thirty-four and was also buried at Westminster: »Here lies Henry Purcell«, is written on his unique epitaph, »Gone to that blessed place where only harmony can be exceeded«. William III died in 1702 after a series of considerable military and political achievements. An intentionally simple and modest funeral procession escorted his remains to Westminster, where he was interred next to his wife in Henry VII's chapel. The century really began with Queen Anne, Mary's sister, with whom William had been reconciled after a few stormy moments. William's coffin bore only the initials of his titles, while Anne's coronation could not have been a particularly solemn occasion because, due to the gout which she suffered, she literally had to be carried to the ceremony. Anne was now able to put Mary II's earlier riposte to the test: as the story goes, during Mary's coronation Anne had maliciously professed pity for her sister queen's fatigue, and Mary replied: »The crown, sister, is not as heavy as it seems«.

The Pantheon of Genius

The eighteenth century was a great period for England and the abbey, even though – with a few exceptions – the *Tory* clergy of Westminster suffered rather than accepted the constitutional monarchy of the Hanoverian kings and the prolonged *Whig* domination. (Dean Francis Atterbury, an influential man of culture and definite *Tory* leanings, was tried for high treason and sent into exile in circumstances which have never been entirely explained). Without losing its privilege as the location for monarchs' coronations and burials, the abbey became most famous for its tombs of great men, at least those who were proclaimed as such for having kept on the right side of the regime. There was no place for transgressors like Jonathan Swift, however, or for those who, like the great poet of that century, Alexander Pope, had no desire to be buried there. Pope was buried in the parish church of Twickenham under a white marble slab which reads: »For one who would not be buried in Westminster Abbey«. As an epitaph, he had dictated the meaningful words: »Heroes and kings, your distance keep!«. This great century was also one of subtle rivalry and intrigue, but this did not prevent Westminster Abbey from becoming a national Pantheon. As such, an unusual visitor, Voltaire, was among those who paid their respects.

One must never forget that during the seventeenth century, the abbey housed many illustrious remains next to those of its kings: Ben Jonson; the poet Abraham Cowley; in 1700, the poet and playwright John Dryden, placed next to Chaucer and accepted despite his conversion to Catholicism. An increasing; y impressive list followed. Military men: commander par excellence, the Duke of Marlborough, whose funeral really did amount to deification. Scientists: Isaac Newton, buried after his body had been solemnly laid out in the Jerusalem Chamber. Politicians: William Pitt the Older and William Pitt the Younger and Charles Fox. Writers of comedies: William Congreve, the leading figure in Restoration comedy; John Gay, author of the *Beggars' Opera*. Actors: David Garrick, the great Shakespearian actor. Scholars: Samuel Johnson, moderator and arbitrator of eighteenth century English education. Other well-known figures, buried elsewhere, from the novelist and comedy writer Oliver Goldsmith to Handel and the famous portrait-painter Godfrey Kneller (who had unwisely said to Pope: »Only fools are buried at Westminster«) were also thought worthy of monuments or tombstones with epitaphs. Goldsmith in fact had the posthumous privilege of a monument by Joshua Reynolds and an epitaph by Johnson.

The epitaphs in the abbey tell a story of their own, and not necessarily because of the solemn thoughts or the emotions they provoke. A typical example is Gay's epitaph, where we read Pope's affectionate, and commemorative verses:

Of Manners gentle, of Affections mild;
In Wit, a Man; Simplicity, a Child:
With native Houmor temp'ring virtuous Rage,
Form'd to delight at once and lash the age:
Above Temptation, in a low Estate,
And uncorrupted, ev'n among the Great:
A safe Companion, and an easy Friend,
Unblam'd thro' Life, lamented in thy End.
These are thy Honours! not that here they Bust
Is mix'd with Heroes, or with Kings thy Dust;
But that the Worthy and the Good shall say,
Striking their pensive Bosoms – Here lies GAY.

This jocular couplet written by Gay himself appears with it:
»*Life is a jest; and all things show it. I thought so once; but now I know it.*«

During all this time, the abbey's western façade, with its towers, was taking on its modern appearance and Westminster became synonymous with the glorification of national heroes. On two occasions, before entering decisive yet uncertain battles, Lord Nelson cried out: »Victory or Westminster Abbey!«. Ironically, this proverbial English hero was not buried at Westminster. He is represented only by a wax statue. Burial in the abbey was denied to the most popular of the Romantic poets, Byron, for reasons which were quite foreseeable if we stop to think about the moral taboos of the time. He was accused of leading a dissolute life, but in any case he had always made it perfectly clear that burial in the abbey was of no interest to him. According to the leading figures of Westminster, there were no preclusions of any kind. In fact, during the seventeeth century, no objections were raised against the unssupulous authorer, Aphra Behn. (Naturally, some limits were not overstepped. When, during the seventeenth century, it was discovered that a headstone was about to be laid on the tomb of a gentleman and well-known seducer, who was murdered by his lover's husband, it was opposed with a firm refusal.) However, the atmosphere of dormancy surrounding the abbey at the beginning of the nineteenth century was an omen of the limitations imposed by Victorian morality. It was not so much a question of ideology, but more to do with the liberal ideas of without doubt the most prominent figure in the abbey during the nineteenth century, Dean Arthur Stanley. He was nevertheless respected because it was recognised that he had his own particular brand of religion, which helps us understand how permission was granted for the burial of Charles Darwin whose *Origin of the Species,* had brought violent accusations of atheism and materialism. His book had been banned in many countries and the teaching of his theory of evolution was forbidden. Nor was there any opposition to the dedication of a tomb in the abbey to the pianist and composer, Muzio Clementi, despite his foreign origin, as well as his reputation as an individual a little too inclined to mix business with pleasure.

The Victorian age, with its spirit, its prejudices and its vitality is reflected in the abbey's history more than any other era. Poetry was represented by the typically Victorian, the poet laureate Alfred Tennyson, a man of be-

liefs and contradictions. A particularly magnificent funeral procession accompanied the comedy writer Richard Sheridan to his tomb. He died in 1816, although his major works were written in the previous century. His pall-bearers were aristocrats with superior-sounding names, even though he died in poverty, without help from any of his powerful admirers. Dickens, the best-known and best-loved writer, requested a modest tomb but even The Times, which had attacked him incessantly during his lifetime, endorsed his burial in the abbey. His grave was prepared early in the morning and, in an unprecedented show of affection, thousands of people attended the funeral. The explorer David Livingstone was buried in the centre of the nave, Stanley's adventurous search for him having become the event of the epoch. On the other hand, like Shakespeare, Keats and Shelley, the Dioscuri of romantic poetry, were commemorated with a monument.

Coronations, with the changes they brought and their loyalty to great traditions, remained the most splendid events taking place in the abbey. »What is the most beautiful sight in the world?« wondered Horace Walpole the scholar, lover of antiquity, writer and author of *Castle of Otranto,* one of the first examples of eighteenth century Gothic novels. »A coronation . . . What do people talk about more than that? Only a coronation. If a puppet show is worth a million, then a coronation definitely is . . .« Walpole's irony was based on his experience as a spectator at Georg II's coronation, a magnificent affair. It was probably the king's intention to accentuate the difference from his father, George I, a Hanoverian monarch with no knowledge of English, who conversed with his ministers in French. His *Premier* Robert Walpole, the writer's father, claimed to have him under his thumb »with bad Latin and a good *punch*«. Horace Walpole thought that the atmosphere at George II's coronation was rather dismal but it suddenly brightened up with some histrionics from the Duke of Newcastle who pretended to cry and faint with emotion. The Archbishop went to his aid, offering a bottle of smelling-salts but then, quite suddenly regaining his strength, he darted about with his lorgnette checking who was there and who wasn't, only to return to his place and bother those near him. Two ladies, notorious ex-lovers of the deceased George I, asked the dean if they could take part in the exclusively male procession singing the praises of the new king. »It was all very enjoyable«, Walpole concluded, »but the most fascinating part was the end«.

The Naked King

The decline of the political and cultural period of history known as Georgian took on an extraordinarily grotesque aspect with the coronation of George IV in 1821. Although it was an historically significant event in the abbey, the events of the ceremony took a political turn for the worse. The king was married to his cousin, Caroline, a German princess who was eccentric to say the least, but her husband was exceptionally harsh with her. The left wing took advantage of the king's matrimonial problems, victimising and blaming the queen. George IV, in turn showing equal disapproval of his wife's undignified behaviour, excluded her from the coronation but feared that she would attempt to force her way in. This is in fact what she tried to do, but without success. The obese George IV, exhausted from the emotion and the heat, perspired profusely during the ceremony and mopped his brow with handkerchiefs which he passed to the equally sweaty primate of England, seated next to him. Judging from reliable sources, the king finally withdrew to a secluded room where he threw himself on the sofa, stark naked with the crown on his head. The history of Westminster Abbey, it seems, does not consist solely of sober events.

It goes without saying that the Victorian age in its turn was epitomised with the coronation of the queen on 28th June 1838. The ceremony, with its mixture of seriousness and comedy, unintentionally took on a Dickensian flavour, although the George II episode was not repeated. The crowd began to gather at dawn in front of the abbey and the guests gradually took their places inside. The dean, who was too old and ill, was not able to take part in the coronation but all the canons were present. Choir-boys dressed in red sang to the accompaniment of an orchestra dressed in scarlet. The ceremony lasted for eight hours, but was completely unrehearsed – »rehearsals« came later and have continued to the present day. The Archbishop was deaf and often missed his cue when it was his turn to recite the ritual phrases. In fact, the ceremony almost came to an abrupt and early end when he skipped two pages of the prayer-book. The ring was too small and the officiant hurt the queen when he tried to force it onto her finger. An old peer tripped on his elaborate gown and almost fell down the stairs, but was stopped in time by the queen. The Archbishop was supposed to hand the orb to the queen in Edward the Confessor's Chapel. However, she had already taken care of this herself which greatly embarrassed the prelate, as the queen herself mentioned afterwards. She was also put out to see that sandwiches and drinks had been laid out for the guests in the Chapel. Disraeli, the famous politician and novelist, wrote that the Prime Minister, Melbourne, was wearing his hat at a slant and brandished his sword »like a butcher«. Nevertheless, Queen Victoria's coronation was more than a traditional ceremony. It provided the English middle classes with the official stamp of respectability to cover up and disguise its dilemmas and problems. The harsh Poor Law had just been proclaimed, the Chartist protest was about to explode and less than ten years later the *Communist Party Manifesto* would appear.

In 1887 Queen Victoria went to Westminster to give thanks and celebrate her fifty years of reign. This ceremony glorifying imperial England was repeated ten years later and Rudyard Kipling appropriately composed a prayer in praise of the country's imperial mission, to which he later added a poem for the coronation of Edward VII. After his mother's impressive funeral ceremony, the new king's different style confirmed that it was the end of an era. The First World War wiped it out definitively even though the empire survived until the Second World War. With the diminishing pomp and ceremony, Westminster Abbey gradually became more of a museum. Kipling and Thomas Hardy were the last great men to have their ashes placed in Westminster,

followed only by the burial of poets laureate such as John Masefield. There would be no interment for great twentieth-century poets and writers like Yeats, T. S. Eliot or Joyce, nor for eminent politicians like Winston Churchill, a descendent of the Duke of Marlborough, whose funeral took place in the abbey. The last great poet to be buried in *Poet's Corner* was Robert Browning, transferred from Italy and placed next to Tennyson who had judged his works obscure. In 1905, the last showman of the English stage, the Shakespearian actor Henry Irving, was interred next to Garrick.

As years passed, the cathedral partly regained a more genuinely religious dimension even though, as we said earlier, its many-facetted image remained that of having lost control of religious piety to the point of making it appear abnormal. George Bernard Shaw shared this point of view when he related the ironic story of the unsuspecting French visitor who was surprised by a sexton while he prayed in the abbey. The sexton was amazed and angered by this unprecedented event and reported him for having disturbed the peace. The judge asked the sexton why one was not supposed to pray in the church, and the good man gave a simple and obvious reply: »If we were to allow this, then we would have people praying all over the place«. The irreverend *enfant terrible* Shaw commented that one could deduce from this that Westminster was for browsing and admiring the monuments, but definitely not for praying.

Almost as symbolic confirmation of its rôle in history, Westminster was affected by both the two great wars of our century. During the First World War, it was slightly damaged by a

German bomb. The damage was more serious, though not irreparable, during the Second World War because of the fires caused by German bombardments. Restoration took many years but the cathedral was ready for Elizabeth II's coronation on 2nd June 1953. Nine hundred years after the consecration of the abbey, the queen took red roses to Edward the Confessor's memorial chapel, and the coronation celebrations lasted for a whole year. However, once again this ceremony was preceded by an unlikely event which to some extent brought back its dramatic past: on Christmas Day 1950, six hundred and fifty years after it had been brought to the abbey, the Stone of Scone mysteriously disappeared. It was a political move, and the political intrigue read like a detective story. The theft was committed by three young Scottish nationalists who hid the precious relic for some months before returning it to Arbroath Abbey in Scotland.

As Edward the Confessor had intended, while maintaining its character and rôle over the centuries, the abbey has become part of a broader area known as the country's political centre, the Houses of Parliament. It is not surprising therefore, that this interchange of religious and civil elements brought about the decision, in 1920, to choose the abbey as the site for the tomb of the unknown soldier, taken from the many nameless tombs on the continent and transferred on the anniversary of the armistice. In the same way, regimental flags have been added over the years. After the Second World War, these included those from the units of fighter planes which, having won the »Battle of Britain«, were a decisive factor in warding off the danger of German invasion. (»Never have so many owed so much to so few, W. Churchill).

Overall, Westminster Abbey is a classical structure influenced by continental Europe, although considered to be a completely original concept and symbol of national culture. The assimilation of different and distinct influences wars the cosmopolitan side of the coin which Joseph Addison extolled during the eighteenth century in a classic article in the »Spectator«. Addison was also solemnly buried in Henry VII's Chapel.

The abbey is a symbol of enduring tradition in a country which had its bloody revolution well before France but, notwithstanding, obstinately maintained an almost uninterrupted continuity in order to preserve its institutions, anachronistic though they may sometimes seem. Leaving aside the eloquence of its national spirit, which cannot be sustained, Westminster Abbey is different from other famous monuments of its kind – for example, Saint Denis in France – because it has never been associated with any specific period in history. It benefited from the legacies of ruling classes succeeding one another throughout the centuries, successfully making it a unique unifying force so that it gradually and irresistibly became the property of the whole nation.

A boss on a vault in Westminster Abbey.

Features and Phases of Construction

The Collegiate Church of St Peter in Westminster – this is the
»abbey's« official title – is one of the most renowned examples
of English Gothic architecture, as testified by the different
chronological phases of its development. An old Benedictine
monastery, the »West Monastery« – hence *West Minster* –
built during the eighth century on the island of Thorney in the
Thames, was perhaps the basis on which the present building
complex was to develop over the centuries. In 1065, King
Edward the Confessor consecrated the first abbey church
which he built on the site of the former Saxon monastery, near
his palace. A few traces of the Saxon and Norman edifices
remain today in the foundations of the buildings adjacent to the
southern arm of the Gothic church's transept. In fact, this was
completely rebuilt by Henry III, starting with the eastern parts,
in accordance with the new, monumental standards of
architectural splendour. It was begun in 1245 and consecrated
in 1269. The combination of the sovereign's refined
»continental« taste and the first master-builder of thirteenth
century construction, Henri de Reynes, probably of French
origin, explains the choice of French Gothic style towards its
completion. Most of the building dates from the second half of
the thirteenth century – apses, transept and the first eastern
spans of the nave – together with the general plan which was
completed later. The building takes the form of the Latin cross,
with a wide, straightforward transept, choir and polygonal apse
with a deambulatory and radial chapels. At about the middle of
the fourteenth century, the western part of the nave was still
»blocked« by the remains of Edward the Confessor's church. It
was completed between the end of the fifteenth and beginning
of the sixteenth centuries when the last seven spans were
erected and the foundations were laid for the bell towers
flanking the entrance. During the early years to the sixteenth
century, the church was enriched with Edward VII's Chapel, a
masterpiece of late Gothic perpendicular, constructed on the
site of the former *Lady Chapel*. The western façade (opposite,
in a painting by Canaletto) was completed in 1734 by
Hawksmoor from a design by Wren.

On these pages, two photographs of the abbey's southern face. Left: the complex system of buttresses and flying-buttresses supporting the length of the building which counterbalance the Gothic structure's load-bearing system (the pillars in the nave and the vaulting ribs) against the perimeter walls. Next to the southern side, the »small cloister« with elegant quadrifoils. Level with the arm of the transept (below), annexes almost completely encompass the buildings.

On the pages which follow, the western façade of the abbey church built in the eighteenth century in Gothic style with the longitudinal axis of the building in an east-west direction. The façade, divided into three parts, mirrors the internal division into three naves. The imposing bell towers »delineated« by angular buttresses, the same width as the aisles, visually and structurally »hold« the nave which is »mirrored« in the façade by the large ogive window in perpendicular style.

The nave (below, looking from the lantern towards the counter-façade) with its mighty vertical upward thrust. It is supported by a complex but perfectly and structurally logical »system« of the framework, and rises to meet the acute arches of the spans and the ribbed vault converging on the carved keystone. The three sections of the nave's wall is comprised, at the base, of pillars and the arches of the nave. The two-tone stone wall continues between the arches.

The triforium runs above the aisles. It is a gallery facing the nave with a succession of ornate mullioned windows with two lights. In Gothic churches these replaced the women's gallery and, therefore, at the highest point the clerestory (from clear and story) large mullioned windows illuminated the nave in addition to the great west window (detail opposite). It was designed during the first decade of the eighteenth century by Sir James Thornhill and made by Joshua Price.

On these two pages are two views of the nave with the »ritual« choir, completely reconstructed in the nineteenth century. Nothing remains of the two much smaller choirs built one after the other during the Middle Ages. The second of these was destroyed in 1774 to be replaced by a new and subsequently destroyed choir designed by the director of works, Keene. The ornate neo-Gothic transenna (or screen) was the work of Blare (1830). There are monuments of Isaac Newton (left) and Lord Stanhope (right) in the two niches flanking the entrance.

Below: detail of the eighteenth century funeral monument to the philosopher and mathematician, Isaac Newton. It was designed by the English architect William Kent and sculpted in the style of Bernini by the Frenchman Louis-François Roubillac. This is one of the many examples of Baroque sculpture in Westminster Abbey, which abounds with funeral and commemorative monuments of that period, especially in the southern transept in Poets' Corner, *and in the northern part which has been set aside as* Statesmen's Aisle.

Opposite: A view of the cross-vault and apses seen from the »ritual« choir. In the foreground we can see the nineteenth-century Gothic style wooden choir-stalls for the choristers. In the background, the sacrarium *or sanctuary with the main altar and carved transenna designed by the architect Gilbert Scott in 1867. This in turn is placed against the fifteenth-century transenna which separated the* sanctuary *from Edward the Confessor's Chapel, entered through the two lateral arches. Above the altar, a mosaic by Salviati of* The Last Supper.

Once we are distracted from the great profusion of detail holding our attention at eye level, we are surprised by the splendour of Westminster's Gothic architecture when we gaze upwards along the outstretched, ascending pillars and pilasters to the perfect harmony of the vaulting. In the nave vaults (opposite) and the aspidal recess (below), the ribs – clearly outlined by light and shadow – complete the elevation visually and logically and reveal the geometrical aspect of the entire architectural design.

In the nave and cross-vault, the dynamic succession of spans with ribbed ogival vaults is arrested by the imposing surrounding pillars and ogival arches of the cross-vault (preceding pages and opposite). This is literally the crucial point of the holy building. In Gothic architecture the ascending framework was emphasised, and this can be seen here in the continuity of the pillars and arches which enclose the »bottomless« lantern. Below: the vaulting of the apsidal recess.

On this page, a detail of the apsidal vaulting. The ribs, converging on bosses carved with gilded leaf motifs, divide and outline the different ceiling segments »filled in« with channels of various coloured stone which, for stability and structural strength, converge in herringbone patterns. Opposite: a view of the northern arm of the transept, called Statesmen's Aisle because of the many commemorative monuments to English statesmen in this part of the church. On the transept's end wall, containing the entrance from the so-called »Solomon's portico« – the double portal decorated externally with much-admired Gothic sculpture – are filled or glazed loggias, while the splendid Gothic rose window contains genuine eighteenth-century stained glass. In fact, it was put up in 1722, at the time of Dean Attenbury, from a design by Sir James Thornhill. It shows the figures of all the evangelists and eleven of the apostles. (The traitor Judas Iscariot was excluded from the usual group).

The almost total destruction of medieval English painting makes
the few thirteenth and fourteenth-century examples kept in
Westminster Abbey, and those originating there but transferred
elsewhere, particularly precious. Opposite: a detail of a
thirteenth-century altar-piece portraying St Peter – in bad
condition and partly obliterated – which decorated Abbot Islip's
Chapel and is today kept in Westminster's Jerusalem Chamber.

As well as the general continental influences widespread in all
English art forms at the time, one can distinguish in this work a
definite trace of Italian Gothic painting similar to that of Duccio
di Buoninsegna. Above: two frescoes, dated around 1300, on the
end walls of the south transept next to the entrance to St Faith's
Chapel, stylistically similar to the altar-piece paintings. Other
medieval paintings, kept today in the British Museum, were
previously in St Stephan's Chapel.

On the opposite page: detail of a fourteenth-century painting of Edward I which decorates the sedilia, the small stalls reserved for the clergy along the southern side of the sanctuary. To the right, the gilded oak coronation throne by Walter of Durham (circa 1300). This holds the legendary Stone of Scone on which the ancient Celtic kings were traditionally crowned. The »Stone of Kings« was brought to London from Scotland in 1296, after a victorious military campaign under Edward I given the title »malleus Scotorum«, (»Hammer of the Scots«) in texts of the period. Since than, the throne has been used for the coronation of English kings. It is usually kept in Edward the Confessor's Chapel but moved to the centre of the sanctuary for coronation ceremonies. Over the centuries, the stone has twice left the abbey: in 1657 when it was transferred to Westminster Hall for the appointment of Oliver Cromwell as Lord Protector, and on Christmas Day 1950 when it was »stolen« by a group of Scottish nationalists.

Behind the main altar is the chapel dedicated by Henry III in memory of the abbey's first founder, Edward the Confessor who died at Westminster in 1066 and was canonised in 1161 by Pope Alexander III. In the centre of the chapel – with its »enclosure« of royal tombs – rises the old shrine of the saint, the true heart of the abbey. Henry III commissioned this from Pietro Oderisi de' Cosmati in Rome, who also laid out the sanctuary floor. A golden reliquary containing the saint's body was originally placed on the stone base. On the opposite page, two details of the inlaid marble Cosmato work. The tomb was dismantled and the reliquary destroyed during the Reformation when religious orders were suppressed, with the resulting ruin of the abbey in 1540. The present reliquary with its graded outlines and more classical style was placed on the old base in 1556 by Abbot Feckenham at the time of the short-lived restoration of Catholicism under Mary I, (Catholic Mary or Bloody Mary).

In the history of English figurative art, the reign of Henry III coincided with a flourishing period of renewed cultural links with the continent. The sovereign, a patron and lover of the arts, brought about the creation of that »court school« of refined and cosmopolitan taste. During the second half of the thirteenth century, the products of this school equalled the finest continental works of art. The oldest royal tombs of Westminster Abbey's deambulatory contain many examples of court sculpture of that period.

On these two pages: a full view and detail of the funeral monument of Henry III's half-brother William de Valence, Lord Pembroke, who died in 1296. It is situated near the rail around St Edward's Chapel. The multicoloured decoration in champlevé enamel on the gilded bronze reclining effigy of the deceased is still in tact. It is one of the best-preserved and most important examples of medieval English court sculpture, which was both rigidly conservative in its form and refined in choice of precious materials and colours.

*Below: a detail of the tomb of Henry III, who died in 1272.
Opposite: a detail of the tomb of Eleanor of Castile, first wife of
Edward I, the Plantagenet, who died in 1290. They are both
works of the London goldsmith William Torel. The reclining
figures in gilded bronze, stylised and elegantly linear, are fairly
detailed. The heads are silhouetted against an enamelled
background of heraldic symbols: the lion of England for the
king, lions rampant and castles with many turrets for Eleanor of
Castile and León.*

47

On the opposite page, the tomb of Edmund »Crouchback«, »the hunchback«, Earl of Lancaster and Henry III's son, who died in 1296. It is located along the southern wall of the sanctuary.
Below: the funeral monument of John of Eltham, Duke of Cornwall and regent of England who died in 1336. This reclining figure in alabaster, a »soft« stone with evocative lustre, is carved with particular attention to detail in the costume and weapons. In the niches along the upper sectors of the side of the base are the mutilated statuettes of the king and queen.

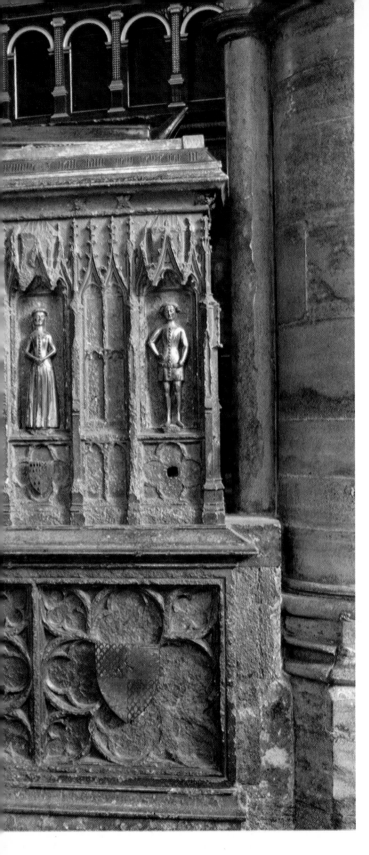

The funeral monument of
King Edward III, who died
alone and forgotten in Sheen
Castle in 1377, is located in
the southern part of the
apsidal deambulatory near
Edward the Confessor's
Chapel. The monument
consists of two blocks of dark
Purbeck marble, placed one
on top of the other and carved
by Henry Yevele. It supports a
reclining gilded copper effigy,
probably the work of the
Englishman John Orchard.
Traditionally, the head was
modelled from a cast taken
directly from the deceased
sovereign's face. It is indeed
very realistic. Six figurines of
weepers are lined up in niches
along the base. These
represent only six of Edward
III and Queen Philippa's
twelve children. The other six
figures on the other side have
disappeared. Each member of
the family has his own small
coat of arms – some removed –
and large, bronze, multi-
coloured enamel coats of arms
representing England and
St George, the royal
prerogative, line the lower
section of the base.

51

The beautiful Gothic doorway to St Erasmus' Chapel (on this page) actually acts as the entrance to St John the Baptist's Chapel. Its original entrance in the apsidal ambulatory has now been totally obstructed by a barrier of funeral monuments. The little chapel, created in the wall-space between two pillars, was probably meant to hold a precious holy image given to the abbey by the wife of Aymer de Valence, who reigned as Richard II during the second half of the fourteenth century. An alabaster statuette of The Virgin with Child now replaces the old statue which has been missing for centuries. Opposite: detail of the funeral monument of Lady Margaret Beaufort, Henry VII's mother who died in 1509. It is situated in the south wing of the chapel which bears her son's name. The monument is by Pietro Torrigiani, the Florentine artist who went to London in 1511 to build the tombs for Henry VII's Chapel, and left nine years later.

Henry VII's Chapel, to which the sovereign paid great attention and enormous sums of money, was constructed between 1503 and 1509 on the site of the former Lady Chapel, *a typical apsidal »appendix« in English Gothic churches in Gothic late-perpendicular style typical of the Tudor period. The new Chapel, rich and refined architecturally and decoratively is subdivided into three aisles by wooden stalls, with each aisle entered by a separate doorway.*

The sepulchres of Henry VII, who died in 1509, and his wife Elizabeth of York, who died in 1502, are located at the end of the nave. The Florentine sculptor Pietro Torrigiani, together with many English assistants, built the monument under the king's detailed instructions and supervision. The reclining gilded bronze figures lie on a black marble base. It is surrounded by an iron grill with the sovereigns' »family« emblems. The details show the Neville greyhound, the Welsh dragon and the French fleur-de-lys.

Below: a view of the entire nave of Henry VII's Chapel, bordered by wooden stalls meant, in 1725, for the Knights of Bath, and over which hang the banners of the Knights Grand Cross of the Order. Opposite: the vault and windows of the apse, with the high stone columns in late perpendicular style. The structure of the vault, supported by a lattice of ribs, is concealed by meticulous fretwork with stars and fans converging on the »pendants« . . .

On the opposite page, a complete view of Mary Queen of Scots tomb. Below: the reclining, white marble statue, carved by Cornelius Cure, of the queen who was beheaded in 1587. It is located in the south aisle of Henry VII's Chapel and forms a pair with the tomb of her cousin and enemy, Elizabeth I in the opposite wing. Both monuments, similar in style and grandeur, were erected by the impartial Stuart James I, son of Mary Queen of Scots, at the beginning of the seventeenth century.

On the opposite page, the funeral monument of Elizabeth I of England who died in 1603, and of her sister and enemy Mary I who died in 1558. They were reunited in the shadow of the marble shrine erected by James I. »Consorts on the throne and in the tomb, here sleep the sisters Elizabeth and Mary, hoping for resurrection«. This is the Latin inscription on the base of the monument, summarising a very complicated saga and »resolving« one of the most bitter and cruel chapters in English history.
The funeral monuments of James I's two children are situated at

the extreme east end of the northern aisle of Henry VII's Chapel, near Elizabeth I's tomb. Sophia, who died when she was three days old in 1606, lies in a brightly coloured coffin like a cradle. Mary, who died aged two in 1607, lies on her side on a marble sarcophagus. Both these monuments, gruesomely »life-like« with the realist accuracy of their heads and the dramatically bright colours, are the work of Maximillian Powtrain.

Opposite: the stained glass windows commemorating the Battle of Britain, at the centre of the apse in Henry VII's Chapel, designed by Hugh Easton and solemnly dedicated by George VI in 1947. Below, in St Paul's Chapel, the tomb of Sir Giles Daubeny, Lord Chamberlain under Henry VII, who died in 1508, and that of his wife Elizabeth. The monument, with reclining alabaster figures, is an important example of the refinement of Renaissance tombs with great attention paid to every detail of the faces and costumes.

On these two pages are three splendidly Baroque Elizabethan tombs. These monuments are characterised by the way the structure is built against the wall, in garishly gilded, coloured marble. The figures of the deceased and their family, portrayed in prayer by the catafalque, are also brightly coloured with the detail of their faces and costumes shown with great accuracy. In this theatrical grouping, the architecture is the »backdrop« and the life-like figures the »protagonists«. Opposite: the magnificent monument erected by Lord Burleigh in memory of his wife Mildred Cecil, who died in 1589, and of his daughter Anna, Countess of Oxford, who died in 1588. The two reclining figures are surrounded by their respective children and grandchildren, while Lord Burleigh, as he wished, is shown at the top of the monument. On this page: top, the funeral monument of Anna, Duchess of Somerset who died in 1587; below, that of Winifred, Marchioness of Winchester who died in 1586.

The Chapter House of Westminster Abbey, entered through a columned vestibule and a double arched doorway from the eastern side of the »little cloister«. It is considered to be one of the marvels of English Gothic. The octagonal building was begun by Henry III in 1250 and probably finished three years later. The load-bearing structure, with its strong, linear ribs, is clearly visible in the central beamed pillar which opens in a fanshaped series of ogival ribs joining the eight perimeter pillars. In this spacious and luminous room, large stained glass windows, placed above a row of trefoil arches behind a marble bench, have almost completely taken the place of walls. Monks sat here during plenary sessions until the dissolution of religious orders under Henry III in 1540. The hall, badly damaged by centuries of neglect, was restored after 1865. The lower part of the walls is decorated with fourteenth and fifteenth-century frescoes portraying the second coming of the Lord on earth and the Apocalypse. The floor, in two-tone terracotta, begun in 1355, is still in good condition (two details, right).

In Gothic architecture, the structure becomes a network of lines
forming the central framework of the building and cancelling
out the load-bearing function of the wall by transferring it to the
»system« of pillars, ogival arches and ribs. In the splendid vault
of the Chapter House (opposite), the load-bearing structure,
with its linear perfection, itself becomes decorative. In a perfect
harmony of stylistic symmetry and structural logic, it is
patterned like a geometrical flower, its petals outlined by the
ribs which open out from the central pillar.

Above: a detail of the blind loggia showing the trefoil arches of
the Chapter House. They are painted with very interesting, if
somewhat damaged, murals. The series (details on the following
pages), by John of Northampton, a monk of the abbey, was
painted during the second half of the fifteenth century in a
primitive style. The different sections and their trompe l'oeil
scrolls with biblical inscriptions illustrate the Apocalypse. The
graphic layout of the narrative makes these paintings seem like
the pages of a beautifully finished book, and the different scenes,
each small and enclosed within its own frame, remind one of the
miniatures on medieval manuscripts.

Dromedary

Bakhepl

Opposite: the deambulatory of the »little cloister«. Its oldest parts date from the period of Henry III. Building continued until mid-fourteenth century when the monks' living quarters were completed. Below, the Chapter House library which occupies part of the monks' old dormitory. It was furnished in its present form in about 1620 by Dean Williams who, at his own expense, filled it with many precious volumes, most of which were lost in the fire of 1694.

Opposite: the Jerusalem Chamber, *near the west entrance to the abbey, once the hall of the abbey's guest-apartments, next to the abbot's residence. This chamber's name probably derives from the subjects of tapestries and paintings which decorated it. Although this room still contains traces of its Gothic origin – the stained glass window with the Beheading of John the Baptist (below), dating from the thirteenth century – it was restored by Dean Williams, whose coat of arms is found above the carved wooden Baroque mantelpiece.*

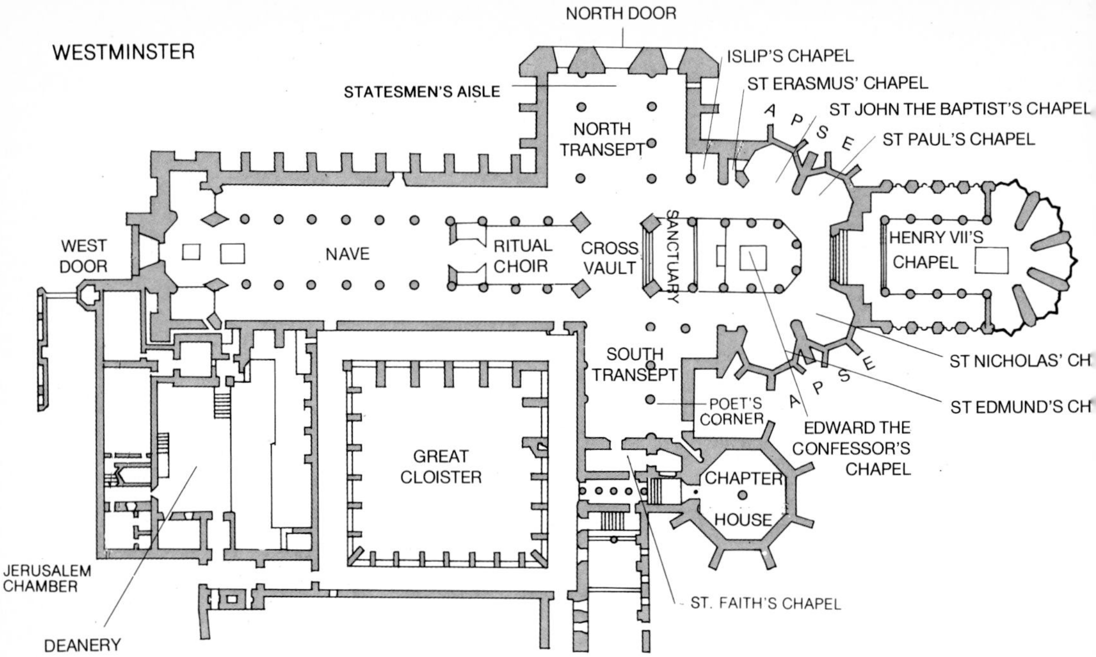
WESTMINSTER
NORTH DOOR
STATESMEN'S AISLE
ISLIP'S CHAPEL
ST ERASMUS' CHAPEL
ST JOHN THE BAPTIST'S CHAPEL
ST PAUL'S CHAPEL
APSE
NORTH TRANSEPT
WEST DOOR
NAVE
RITUAL CHOIR
CROSS VAULT
SANCTUARY
HENRY VII'S CHAPEL
SOUTH TRANSEPT
POET'S CORNER
GREAT CLOISTER
CHAPTER HOUSE
EDWARD THE CONFESSOR'S CHAPEL
ST NICHOLAS' CH
ST EDMUND'S CH
JERUSALEM CHAMBER
DEANERY
ST. FAITH'S CHAPEL

Index

WARNER MEMORIAL LIBRARY
EASTERN UNIVERSITY
ST. DAVIDS, PA 19087-3696